KT-572-505

Wedding Speeches & Toasts

CASSELL ILLUSTRATED

First published in the UK in 1994 by Ward Lock as
Wedding Speeches and Toasts

This revised and updated edition published in 2006
by Cassell Illustrated
A division of Octopus Publishing Group Ltd
2–4 Heron Quays
London E14 4JP

Text and design copyright © 2006 Cassell Illustrated
Revised and updated by Nick Marshallsay and Jane Moseley

A CIP catalogue record for this book is available from the British Library.

ISBN-13: 978-1-844035-20-5
ISBN-10: 1-844035-20-4

Printed and bound in the United Kingdom

Contents

Introduction

Making a speech at a social occasion is often thought to be worse than having to stand up and speak at a business function. Not being able to enjoy the occasion for fear of embarrassing yourself in front of family and friends, is many peoples' worst nightmare. But whatever your role, be it father of the bride, groom, best man or chief bridesmaid, don't panic. This book contains samples of speeches for every part of the wedding from engagement parties to stag and hen nights to the wedding itself, whether a traditional 'white' wedding, or a more alternative ceremony.

People make speeches at weddings to express thanks, give information and, quite simply, because it is a tradition. You also have a unique opportunity to pay public compliments to those you love. However, as with any speech-making, there are certain things to avoid when giving a speech at a wedding:

* Don't allow yourself to be overwhelmed by the concept of 'making a speech'. Instead, think of it rather as welcoming supportive, friendly people to the event and entertaining them for a few minutes – a sort of extended conversation that just happens to be with a larger than usual group of people.

- Don't leave things to the last minute, and, unless you have a special gift for excellent and improvised public speaking, make sure you prepare what you are going to say well in advance.

- Don't underestimate your audience or, indeed, overestimate them – in age, experience, tolerance and understanding of your language or humour. Not everyone will be as familiar with the family history as you. There may be grannies and children present, so if using humour, keep it appropriate.

- Don't look down when you talk, don't whisper and don't shout, don't swear too much and don't improvise unless you feel really confident.

- Don't make your speech a series of loosely connected quotations from famous or other people. If you have written your own poem, don't perform it unless it has been read and vetted first.

- Don't forget that this speech is about the occasion and your relationship to the person/people involved. It is not a speech about you. It is not a vehicle for self-promotion or an audition for a reality show. Don't confuse 'eye contact' with 'I contact'.

chapter 1

Planning, Writing & Practising your Speech

When first sitting down to write your speech it may be a good idea to ask yourself why you have been asked to speak. Is it because you are expected to express good wishes or thanks, or because you are old and wise and expected to give advice, or because you are an extrovert and known for being humorous, because you are closely related to other members of the family, or because you are a friend who has known the bride and bridegroom for many years? The answer to this question may suggest to you what sort of speech to give. There may also be certain things that you will be expected to say – as a best man, you will need to thank the bridesmaids, and as the groom you will have to thank your new parents-in-law. Have a look at pages 44–45 to find out what these are.

Planning your speech

It is important to leave yourself enough time before the wedding in order to give as much consideration as possible to what you would like to say and to do any research necessary, as well as to write your speech and to perform any last-minute pruning. Remember, a few scribbled notes will not suffice.

Length of speech

Decide how long your speech needs to be before you begin to research and write it. Too short and it may seem rude, too long and it may bore the guests and dampen the proceedings. If you really can't decide, settle on about five minutes. As a rule of thumb, if the occasion is a very formal one it will demand a longer speech; an informal occasion is more flexible. Remember, your speech will reflect not only on those you are speaking about, but upon yourself.

Gathering information

Before even attempting to write your speech, take stock of the information you have to hand and see where the gaps occur. Only then should you set about researching in order to fill your speech out, make it interesting, witty, or whatever style of speech you would like to make. Beware, however, of drowning yourself in pages of notes. Panic will not be too far away if, having collected all your information, you have only a little time to write the speech.

Begin your research by looking for ideas on which you can expound and expand. For instance, the theme of marriage itself is always popular. You could research ideas on the history of marriage and interesting marriage customs both here and abroad.

In addition, you could ask the parents of the bride and bridegroom about their marriages. Did the marriage take place in wartime? Wearing similar clothes? With hundreds of guests? Enquire about the cake, photographer, transport, food, music, dancing, honeymoon destination, and first home. The grandparents, uncles and aunts may also have interesting stories about their weddings and the marriages of friends, brothers, sisters and other relatives that took place in unusual or typically different circumstances in earlier days.

The best time to get people to talk about themselves is when you are sitting around the table over a meal or having tea, and when they are relaxed and are not likely to be diverted by other activities. Remember here that some people do not like seeing you write down their words, since it interrupts their flow of thought. If you have a poor memory you could slip away for a moment and write yourself a quick note. Alternatively, use a small tape recorder so that you can join in the conversation without note-taking. Reactions to tape recording differ. While a few people do not like tape recorders, others love to have what they said played back at a family party, and then argue and correct each other and make interesting extra comments.

From the family history you can learn about the family's ancestors, where they have lived and worked, where they met, their education, work skills, achievements, hobbies and character. Personal anecdotes can be added. You will need to strike a balance between personal and general remarks. For example, if the bride and bridegroom have fascinating family histories, it would be unfortunate if you generalized a great deal and delivered a speech that could have been given at anybody's wedding.

So make sure you persist even if your first enquiry produces no immediate result. You may find that the bride says: 'Don't bother to say anything about where I went to school and where we met. It's not really interesting.' If one of your subjects doesn't provide you with information, ask another. You might discover that someone else such as the bride's mother has really interesting revelations about the bride. Maybe despite or because of failing 'O' levels, she went on to become the first woman engineer at her college because her earlier setbacks had made her determined to prove that she could succeed.

Make enquires from both sides of the family. The discovery of the meaning of the family name may be news to the other side. And the countries all the grandparents came from could be quite interesting. But so is the fact that one or both families have lived in the same area for four generations. This is not the sort of news that would make the front pages of newspapers, but you can assume that on the day everyone will be interested in the bride and bridegroom and their respective families.

The profession of the bride or bridegroom may provide speech matter. If your subject has academic qualifications you could ask such questions as: 'How long did it take you to get your degree?'; 'What subject is your PhD in?'; 'How long have you been a member of the Architect's Association'; 'Where did you study for the Bar?'; 'How does the FBOA differ from the FSMC?'.

If the bride or bridegroom, or their families or ancestors, are famous, it might be worth your while looking them up in Who's Who, and similar reference works, of which there are many editions covering authors, scientists, theatrical personages and royalty.

Writing your speech

The first draft

Choose a time of day when you can work without inter-ruption. Sit down and start writing, using any collated material that appeals and which you think is relevant. If a fact or an idea reminds you of a story, write it down. At this early stage you can allow your mind the freedom of expression. Whether or not you use all the material written at this time is not so important. The crucial factor is to get started and to create. The imagination may be inhibited if too many boundaries are introduced too early.

Develop the habit of writing in the way in which you speak, because it is you that your audience wants to hear. It may also help your ideas to flow more easily.

The second draft

This is the stage at which you groom your speech – you may need to rewrite your existing material. In the original draft you tapped your creative skills by permitting your-self to think broadly about your subject. Now you can afford to discipline your work and thus build a format, without being in danger of losing the heart of your speech and the spontaneity of your ideas.

Keep the audience at the back of your mind as you prepare your second draft – remember what the groom's friends might find amusing, the bride's mother might not think quite so funny. Consider also whether you have guests who are not fluent in English (see also page 42), for example, if the bridegroom is of a different nationality.

Will you have an interpreter to translate for you or will the listeners just be expected to keep up? Either way, keep your language simple and be careful not to use too many colloquialisms. Remember ideas of humour can vary between cultures; it's not a good idea, for example, to make a joke about the French if the groom's mother and some of the guests are French – regardless of your good intentions and how funny you think it is, it could be taken as an insult. Similarly, avoid jokes that rely on word play and double entendres as these could be lost in translation or not understood by those who don't have English as their first language.

Because you have written the first draft, most of your material and the substance of your speech are probably all there, and just need to be moulded into shape. If you decide to work on the middle of the speech first, remember that it needs to be arranged so that it flows smoothly. A well-structured speech is like a chain, with one link fastened to the next. A speech written with this in mind will flow and put the audience at their ease. They will relax and so be able to concentrate more easily on what is being said.

Keep your speech simple without appearing patronizing or condescending. Be direct, positive and to the point without any abruptness. The syntax can influence the way a speech is delivered, so write it in a warm manner that can be translated into cheerful speech. Add a little colour by telling a story or an appropriate quote or joke (see Chapter 6 for some ideas). This can also help to re-engage flagging interest.

Before you begin, reread your first draft and then:

- Prune your notes if necessary and arrange them in the correct order. List the essentials to be included such as thanks and the toast. Then consider your opening remarks.

- Avoid stereotyped ideas if possible. Have you talked only about the bride cooking for the bridegroom when you know she is a career girl and a women's libber, and even if she is not, some of the audience could be?

- Delete anything in dubious taste. If in doubt, leave it out. Avoid negatives, regrets, criticisms of others, making the families or yourself appear foolish and anything vague.

- Remove rude jokes and deliberate sexual innuendos, and watch out for unintended double entendres that might make inebriated members of the audience laugh when you are being serious and sincere. You can cause hysterics all round with such apparently innocent remarks as the bride's father saying: 'I didn't expect to enjoy myself so much. You don't enjoy things so much when you get older.'

When the second draft is completed, put it away in a drawer and forget it for a few days. Come back to it later and view it afresh. This is the time to edit your speech and delete unnecessary material. Remember that a short, well-structured speech is preferable to one that is longer but less memorable.

Reading your speech aloud

Read the speech aloud to yourself to be sure the sentences are not too long and you are not stumbling over them. It must sound like something you would say spontaneously. Later when you are satisfied, you might read it to a limited number of people – just one or two. You don't want all the wedding party to have heard the speech in advance of the wedding. Alternatively, you could tape-record your speech, listen to it and criticize yourself. This is also a good opportunity to time it and make any alterations in length or pace of delivery.

Improving the style

Change words or phrases you have repeated. Enliven clichés by subtly altering them if possible. Explain jargon and foreign phrases.

Change repetitions by looking for new words with the same meaning in a thesaurus. A dictionary of synonyms and antonyms might also be useful. And if you intend to compose your own poems, limericks or verses, a songwriter's rhyming dictionary would be invaluable.

For an ordinary wedding, a colloquial way of speaking will be suitable. However, should you be called upon to speak at a grand, formal wedding you may feel that a more erudite speech is required. Forms of address and titles for important personages can be found in reference books.

To eliminate or locate colloquial words there are dictionaries of slang. For transatlantic marriages, several dictionaries of American expressions are available,

enabling you to eliminate Americanisms, explain yourself to American listeners, or make jokes about the differences between Americanisms and conventional
English language.

Anticipating little problems

Try to anticipate any controversial subjects and disasters
you might have to mention, or avoid mentioning, in the
course of your speech.

Make yourself a troubleshooter's checklist.
What would I say if:

• Her father had recently died?

• His or her parents couldn't or didn't attend?

• The best man didn't arrive because his plane from
  India was delayed?

• It turned out to be the bridegroom's second wedding,
  although it is the bride's first?

• The chief bridesmaid didn't turn up because she was
  ill?

• The bridegroom dried up and forgot to compliment
  the bridesmaids so I couldn't thank him?

• You may also have to state facts that are obvious to
  you, but would not be to distant cousins.

Final check

Finally, check that your speech fits in with the speeches and toasts given by others. Be sure that you know the name of the previous speaker so that you can say: 'Thank you, George', confident that his name is not James. And if the bridegroom, the bride's father or another older man is usually called 'Al', on this occasion should you be calling him by his full name (and if so, is that short for Albert, Alfred, Ali, Alexis, Alexander) or, even more formally, Mr Smith?

Run a few questions past yourself about your speech:

- Will everyone understand and appreciate the content?

- Will the guests have heard all my jokes before?

- Will my speech give offence or repeat what others have said?

- Did people laugh/fall asleep during the rehearsal?

- Do I know my speech well enough?

- Have I worked out how long it will last?

Preparing a speech to read

It is best to avoid the temptation of memorizing a speech. It is much easier to forget lines than to forget the gist of what you wish to say. Forgetting a word or sentence can throw some people and undermine their confidence. Familiarizing is better than memorizing. It allows the speaker's personality to come into focus and the speech will sound more spontaneous. There are two ways of preparing your speech to read – either by using extended notes and phrases to jog your memory, or by using prompt cards.

Using notes and phrases

If you aren't comfortable with the idea of reducing your speech to fit onto prompt cards, here are some hints for using notes and phrases to deliver your speech:

- Rewrite your second draft in phrases and group them by ideas or in pairs.

- Provide a good space between each phrase. This avoids confusion and marks the end of one idea and the start of another. This enables you to look at the audience regularly and return to your place with ease.

- Write as you would speak and avoid the use of too many abstract concepts. Use pictorial language when the opportunity presents itself.

- Use a black pen on white paper and keep the writing quite large. Or, if printing from the computer, use a large point size and double-line spacing.

Prompt cards

However, there is another way. Many speakers transcribe the main topics of the material onto postcards. These are known as prompt cards. They enable you to refer to major points that will serve as cues during your delivery.

It can be hard to relinquish pages of well-researched information in exchange for small rectangles of cardboard, each of which holds no more than a few headings. You may think you will never remember anything from them and the first time you attempt to rehearse your speech, your confidence can take a nosedive as you realize your worst fears.

This can be the danger period: the transition from paper to card – that reluctant surrendering of reassuring sheaves of rustling paper. Try to see this as a testing time and, if you can, persevere and use the cards. Once you make that breakthrough you will go from strength to strength.

Preparing prompt cards

If you decide to use cards, here are some suggestions for layout:

- Use one side of the card only.

- Number each one clearly with a black or coloured pen.

- Don't try to cram more than the essentials onto the postcard, or you may spend much of the speech peering at details that have been written in tiny handwriting.

- Insert any vital information that will need careful reference.

- The cards may be separate or strung together, whichever is the more comfortable.

Once you have done this, practise. That way you will improve and gain confidence. You will be able to look at the audience while you speak and communication will be at its strongest.

Here is a simple example of a prompt card from a father of the bride:

Sarah growing up
Baby – pram story
At school – missing school report
As a teenager – party at our house

Remember that familiarity breeds content! Once your notes have been pruned to postcard headings, rehearse your speech as often as you feel the need. So make a friend of your speech and have fun rehearsing – the key thing is to practise!

Using a microphone

When you arrive at the wedding reception check whether a microphone will be available. But be prepared and able to speak without it just in case it is not available or an electrical fault develops.

At a seated dinner the speakers are usually at the top table and the microphone is nearby and can be handed to each speaker. But if the first speaker is not seated at the top table there may be a pause while he walks to the microphone. If a delay occurs between one speaker and the next the audience may start talking so that the next speaker will have to recapture their attention. A toast-master has his own techniques. He may bang on the table with a mallet and then shout: 'Pray silence for THE BRIDE-GROOM!'

The first speaker should not be the one who discovers whether the microphone is working or not. Perhaps the best man could take on the responsibility of arriving before the guests and checking the microphone. However, the best man is sometimes asked to stay behind at the church, organizing transport and ensuring that the last guest does not get stranded when all the cars have departed. In this case another usher or bridesmaid could take over the duty of checking the microphone.

The usual technique for checking that the microphone is set to the correct level after the audience arrives is to call: 'Can you all hear me?' Since those at the front shout loudly, you won't necessarily know that those at the back can't. A more interesting variation would be: 'Hello, I'm going to check that the microphone works before I start. Could those on the back table shout, 'Hello'.' Another variation would be: 'Hello, I just want to check you all got here all right. Did the relatives from Manchester arrive?' (Check the table plan in advance to see who is on the back table or tables.) 'Yes? Good. Now I can start.'

When you begin speaking into the microphone, start softly and then speak louder. You don't want to start by bellowing so loudly that people shrink in alarm. If you see the audience cowering back, you are too loud. Alternatively, see if they are straining to hear you. Some experienced speakers ask a friend to stand against the back wall and signal with hands facing forward by their ears if you need to speak louder, and with hands horizontal if you should speak more softly.

Ensure that you are not so near the microphone that it picks up every sound, including heavy breathing and muttered asides. Neither stand so far away that it cannot pick up your voice. The other thing to avoid is swaying backward and forward so that you are alternately bellowing and whispering, fading out or disappearing entirely at intervals like a badly tuned radio station!

Don't be frightened that you are speaking too loudly. Everybody wants to hear you because they are your friends, or because they are friends of the happy couple and want to hear what you have to say about them. If you practise listening to yourself speaking on tape, you will be used to the timbre or magnification of your voice.

chapter 2

Pre-wedding Speeches

There are several occasions that are likely to arise prior to the wedding itself at which a speech might be required. One of these is an engagement party, arranged to introduce families and friends, and inform everyone that the couple are now attached. If the engagement period is to be protracted because the couple are young or studying, there may be a big party not unlike a small-scale version of the wedding at which the future bride has a chance to display her ring to well-wishers and acquire presents for the new home, for which the guests must be thanked. The other times when speeches are often called for before a wedding are bachelor and hen parties, held in the weeks just prior to the wedding, when the friends of the bride and groom gather together to give them a good send-off into married life.

More than one bride's father has been heard to say that he did not want to have a large engagement party if the wedding was to follow within a year because that would involve him in the organization and expense of 'two weddings'. That is why the bridegroom's family traditionally hosts the engagement party, but there is no reason why one should not be held by the bride's family, or by both families in their own homes or elsewhere, particularly if the two families live in different areas.

Unlike wedding reception speeches, the engagement party speeches are usually very short, merely introducing the young couple, expressing pleasure at the engagement and wishing them happiness. A parent of the bride or bridegroom speaks or, if there are no parents present, another older relative playing host can make the speech.

Impromptu speeches

It's possible that you might be called upon to make a speech at such an occasion without any warning. For those well versed in the art of public speaking this may not be difficult; for the novice it can be nerve-wracking. Always be prepared for the unexpected. If you think that you might at some stage be asked to 'fill in', take time to jot down a few notes (with the key points on cards) that can be used in an emergency. This is particularly appropriate if you feel that you are not good at thinking on your feet. Keep a notebook of amusing jokes and anecdotes or use the space at the end of this book. Practise rehearsing one or two of these from time to time. This will prepare you for that unexpected invitation.

There are two great tools to support impromptu speeches: these are structure and storytelling.

Structure

The 'tell 'em' structure: Tell 'em what you're going to tell 'em, tell 'em, tell 'em what you've told 'em. When asked to make impromptu speeches, speakers can feel out of control if they have no framework within which to set their thoughts. The 'tell 'em' structure can be used in many situations, such as when standing up at short notice in front of a group.

In the example below, the best man has a simple structure to keep the speech focused and prevent a rambling discourse.

Example: Impromptu speech by a best man at a bachelor party:

'We're all here because we are good friends of Steven, and we want to wish him all the best before he heads off into married life. Steven, you're a great friend, and Annabelle is a lucky girl to be spending the rest of her life with you, although some here (who shall remain nameless) would say that it's the other way round and that you're the lucky one to have found someone who will put up with your love of football/cricket/cars/terrible music! So let's all raise our glasses to Steven. To Steven!

Storytelling

If you were the best man and were suddenly called upon to give a speech on the groom, it could seem daunting. What is difficult is that we have a lot of information in our head, but no planned format for its delivery. One way, as we have seen above, would be to use some structure, so that we could talk about his family, his school days, his hobbies and then his career in order to give ourselves direction. The other alternative would be to tell a simple story about your experiences of the subject:

Example: Impromptu speech about Steven using story-telling

'To tell you a little about Steven and his attitude to life, I'd like to take you back to when we were 14 at school together and went on the school French trip to Elbeuf in Normandy'...

Engagement parties

Engagement parties aren't the occasion for long speeches. A lot of the people present will also be guests at the wedding, so save your stories about the bride and groom for then.

Engagement party speeches
Speech to the happy couple by the bridegroom's (or the bride's) father/mother:
'I am delighted to welcome you to meet Steven's fiancée Annabelle and her family [or Annabelle's fiancé Steven and his family]. It is lovely to see so many friends. I hope everybody's got a glass of champagne because I would like you to join me in wishing happiness to Annabelle and Steven. [Pause]
To Annabelle and Steven.'

Reply and thanks to the host and guests by bride/ bridegroom and toast to the other family:
'I want to thank Mum and Dad for throwing this lovely party so that you could meet Annabelle and her family [or Steven and his family]. Thank you all for coming this evening, and for bringing such generous presents. I'd like you to drink a toast to Annabelle's parents, Betty and Jim [or Steven's parents, John and Clare]. [Pause]
To Betty and Jim [or John and Clare].'

Thanks and toast to hosts by the other family:
'I'd like to thank Betty and Jim for organizing this wonderful party to give both of our families the ideal opportunity to get to know each other.'

Bachelor parties

Stag and hen parties used to be held the night before the wedding, the last opportunity for the girls and boys to go out with friends of their own sex. Now, however, the occasionally unfortunate results of these parties have made it unpopular to hold them immediately before the wedding, and instead a date a couple of weeks earlier is chosen.

The responsibility of the brother, sister or best friend who organizes the bachelor party is to ensure that it is a happy event for the guest of honour, and that the speeches, jokes, entertainment and gifts do not embarrass those present or others absent who will hear about the party later, or imperil the relationship between the engaged couple. Organizing the event successfully, making an amusing speech, and getting the right balance between outrageous fun and good taste will indicate to the bride or bridegroom that you can be relied upon to perform well as best man or bridesmaid at the subsequent wedding.

Bachelor and hen party speeches
Speech to bridegroom-to-be by best friend:

'We are here to say goodbye to our brother, Steven, who is departing for the land of the married. We all knew that Steven was regarded as an eligible bachelor, but we didn't think that marriage was what he was eligible for. We tried to dissuade Steven from marrying, but alas to no avail. We warned him that a husband is a glorified handyman, that he will be spending his weekends painting, decorating, gardening and maintaining the car. He will be abandoning happy Saturday afternoons spent watching football, and instead spend them shopping. If he cannot afford a dish-washer, he will be a dishwasher. Sunday will no longer be a day of rest spent playing cricket or sailing, but devoted to visiting in-laws. Evenings at the pub or the bar will have to be abandoned and he will stay at home, opening bottles for others to drink. To all this, he said, and I quote: 'Rubbish.' So you see, his vocabulary has changed already! He continued: 'You are not married. How do you know?'

So we sought wiser men than ourselves who have trodden the same path he proposes to take. W.C. Fields said that women are like elephants, very nice to look at, but he wouldn't want to own one. A look at our former friends who have married will show that 'marriages are made in heaven above, to make life hell below.' [Alternatively choose a quotation from the selection in Chapter Six.] Many young ladies will mourn Steven's departure. Sometimes they were queuing up to speak to him. In fact, a lady who looked like Britney Spears [or other celebrity the groom is known to admire] was hiding in the phone box at the car park waiting to see him as we came along tonight. She is still waiting, alas in vain.

We, too, have failed. He remains unconvinced. To him, an evening with one woman, Annabelle, is worth an evening with ten of us. She must be a truly wonderful girl. We shall never know. So we have gathered here this evening to spend a last evening telling jokes with our friend, while he is unfettered by responsibilities. We decided to present him with a small token that he can take to his new life, and keep in memory of his bachelor days and the friends he has left behind. Unfortunately, when we went into the shop to buy his gift we met a couple of his ex-girlfriends who insisted on coming along to remind him of the girls he is leaving behind, and to present him with a small, but wonderfully packaged gift, a token of our friendship. Steven – here they are!'

[At this stage, two male friends dressed in drag appear, possibly as twin brides, preferably in long dresses or other outfits that keep them well covered to prevent any incidents among their own group or from outsiders. They present the gift.]

Reply and thanks by the bridegroom-to-be:

'Dear Friends. I appreciate your concern for me. I, too, am concerned for you. Your gifts are very welcome and will be appreciated by Annabelle as well as myself. Boys [Guys/Mates], you don't know what you are missing. While I am tucked up by my warm fire being waited on hand and foot, you will be out in your cars touring the streets with nowhere to go, wishing in vain for a lovely girl to console you and end your loneliness.

How can a football or a golf ball be compared to a girl? Those of you who still do not know the difference, I hope will one day find out. In only five weeks I shall be marrying Annabelle. We look forward to seeing you all at our wedding, and later to welcoming you to dinner in our new home. Who knows, at the wedding or at our place you may meet the girl who may change your mind about the joys of remaining a bachelor. Annabelle and I have got a 'little list' of eligible bachelors, and you are all on it. We have had many good times together, and we shall have more. I am not halving my friends, but doubling them. Please raise your glass and drink a toast to Alan who has organized this party for me. May he enjoy happy bachelor days, but not too many, before he realizes the error of his ways and is claimed by his own beautiful lady. [Pause] To Alan.' [An alternative toast could be to friendships that endure forever.]

Speech to bride-to-be by best friend:
'We tried to dissuade Annabelle from marrying, but alas to no avail. We warned her that a wife's work is never done. She is chained to the kitchen sink and washing socks. Unpaid secretary, social organizer, babysitter, cook, etc. When we told her this she said, and I quote: 'Phooey!'

There are many young men who will mourn her departure from the ranks of the available, ah [sigh], some of whom had fond memories of her, others, merely hopes. She was a very popular girl. Men flocked into her office. We realized why when we called. She had taken the sign MEN from the gents and put it on her office door. But now that Steven has claimed her, those days are gone. Her parents and flatmates look forward to the recovery of their telephones and bathrooms.

We must admit that it looks to us like a very good match, and it is only because she is marrying Steven that she has such an idealized view of what men and marriage are really like. Does she not know the truth, that after marriage, life changes. Men can be late. Women cannot. We are duty bound to warn her of what others who married have said. But since we have failed to persuade her to stay single, we can only wish her well, and give her this small token of our good wishes for her future, in memory of our happy single days together.' [Produce appropriate gift.]

Reply and thanks by the bride-to-be:

'Dear friends. I appreciate your message of goodwill, and your charming gifts. Don't you dare tell Steven that you found this pair of men's underpants/bottle of tequila/Michael Jackson record under my bed! I shall always remember you, the way you look tonight! We have had a lot of fun together and we still shall. You'll all be at my wedding in six weeks/six months time, and frequent guests at my house. I shall throw my bouquet to one of you at the wedding and who knows, there might be another wedding in the not too distant future for some-body – my mother says there's one for everyone. So let's all have a drink together – I hope all my girlfriends will meet steady boyfriends, but as Helen organized this party and is going to be my chief bridesmaid, I'd like to wish happiness to Helen. To Helen.' [An alternative toast would be: 'To friendship. May good friends stay together forever'.]

chapter 3

Wedding Etiquette and Timings

W hat is a speech and what is a toast? You can have a speech without a toast, and a toast without a speech, but at a wedding it is usual to combine the two.

Traditionally, the first speech, usually given by the bride's father or an old family friend, ends with the proposal of a toast to the health of the bride and bridegroom. The second speech is given as a reply to the first by the bridegroom and is concluded with the proposal of a toast to the bridesmaids. The best man then replies on behalf of the bridesmaids, and will conclude his speech by proposing a toast to the parents of the bride and bridegroom. And remember, women are increasingly being asked to take on the role of 'best man', so there is no need to feel awkward or unusual! So, throughout, read 'best man' to mean best man or woman.

The modern wedding, however, is flexible and the bride may feel comfortable making the speech on behalf of herself and her new husband, for example. Or the job of replying to the toast of the bridesmaids could be taken on by the chief bridesmaid rather than the best man. The bride may be given away by her mother, who can also speak if she so wishes.

Etiquette

The purpose of etiquette is to provide an easy set of rules that we can follow when we are in a hurry and want to make sure that we do not give offence to anybody. For example, we would not wish to neglect to thank the hosts, or fail to recognize the presence and importance of an honoured guest. The rules are most useful on formal occasions like weddings, particularly when they happen only once in a lifetime. But because lifestyles are changing constantly, the rules of etiquette are changing, too. However, these should give you a basic idea of what to do and say.

The timing of the speech

Circumstances vary and the rules of speechmaking differ for different religions. When speeches are made after seated dinners at lengthy, formal wedding receptions, they begin after all eating at the formal meal has finished, and are preceded by the announcement from the toastmaster: 'Ladies and Gentlemen, you may now smoke.' If the meal finishes with tea or coffee and wedding cake, speeches will be made after the cutting of the cake.

However, if the celebration is to continue all evening and the tea or coffee and wedding cake are to be served later, it is possible to delay the cutting of the cake until after the speeches that conclude the meal. Whatever the wedding organizers decide, it is important to let the toastmaster and the speechmakers know, so that they are prepared and do not disappear at the vital moment.

You might have late guests arriving after the wedding meal, as the number of guests invited to the meal was limited by the cost or the size of the hall. Sometimes the seated guests are just the closest family and friends, while other friends, children, neighbours and work colleagues are invited later for the dancing and party. A few guests who are invited to a midweek ceremony may not be able to leave work early, are delayed by rush hour traffic, or have to return home to change their clothes, and therefore they reach the reception after it has started.

Guests should not enter during the speeches, distracting the audience and disconcerting the speakers. But it is also necessary to avoid keeping them standing outside in the rain, or waiting in draughty corridors feeling unwanted while the meal finishes or the speeches are in progress. The hotel or hall staff can arrange chairs, drinks, and someone to direct and greet the late arrivals, who can then view the wedding presents, or be introduced to each other until a suitable moment arrives for them to enter the dining hall. They should then not be left standing if the other guests are seated, but shown to chairs on one side of the hall, or be directed to the seating plans so that they can fill the places kept for them, or go to seats left empty by 'no-shows' such as anyone taken ill at the last minute. You may wish to time the cake cutting and speeches so that later arrivals can enjoy them. The printed invitation can make any such timing clear.

Buffets and informal weddings

At a buffet, ensure that elderly and infirm guests, and those who have travelled long distances, have seats near the buffet table so that they won't have to stand for a long time. If there is no toastmaster, the best man calls for attention for the start of the cake-cutting ceremony. The bride and bridegroom pose for photographs to be taken by the official photographer and guests who have brought their cameras. The chief bridesmaid, if she is not making a speech, can then lead the call for a speech.

The toastmaster

The first question you need to ask yourself is: do you need a toastmaster? At a large wedding it is usual to have a toastmaster to announce guests on the receiving line. He will know the traditional way to announce titles, that Mr and Mrs John Smith are husband and wife, Mrs John Smith is attending without her husband John, Mrs Anne Smith is a widow, or that Mr John Smith and Miss Anne Smith are the elderly aunt and uncle, brother and sister, not married to each other. The toastmaster opens the proceedings and keeps them flowing smoothly. In his absence the task would fall to the best man.

There are other benefits from employing a toastmaster. Since one essential quality of a good toastmaster is a loud voice (which often goes with an imposing, extrovert personality), they will get attention quickly (an alternative way to get the attention of the audience is to ask the band, if you have one, to do a drum roll for you). To ensure that proceedings go as you would wish, give the toastmaster instructions in advance, rather than piecemeal later.

If a toastmaster attends, he will begin his duties by announcing the guests stepping forward to shake hands with the bridal party on the receiving line. Afterwards he will raise his voice and shout loud enough to be heard by the whole roomful of guests, 'LADIES and GENTLEMEN! Pray be seated. DINNER is now being served!' When everyone has found their places he stands by the microphone at the top table, hammers on the table with a gavel and announces loudly: 'Ladies and Gentlemen, Pray SILENCE for the Reverend John Smith, who will now say grace.'

If there is no toastmaster, the best man may introduce the minister more simply: 'Ladies and Gentlemen, Reverend John Smith will now say grace.' He should check in advance the correct title and form of address for the minister, Archbishop, Chief Rabbi, or whoever will be attending.

Surprise announcements

The surprise delivery of a gift, or the surprise arrival of a friend or relative from overseas, can be fun. However, the best man or chief bridesmaid will have to take responsibility for the announcement, and the safe-keeping of any gift. Most gifts are sent to the home of the bride's mother in advance. That way the donor's cards are not muddled during the day, and presents are kept safely and not left in hotels or halls where they might go astray.

Bear in mind too that it is the bride's day, and surprise announcements of the engagements and weddings of other guests might deflect attention from the bride. The announcement of the engagement of the bride's sister would be acceptable if the bride herself knows in advance and agrees to it being made at her wedding.

Informal receptions

If your wedding guests are not seated in a reception hall, but milling around a hotel or house your problem is to ensure that everyone is gathered in the right place at the right time to hear the speeches. You may have to tell guests in advance: 'We're cutting the cake and having the speeches in the dining room at half past', then send the chief bridesmaid into the gardens if it is a fine day, and the other bridesmaids around the house, to inform stragglers that the speeches are about to be made.

Don't start the proceedings until you are sure that the speakers themselves are present as well as the hosts and anyone else who will be thanked or mentioned in the speeches. Keep the speeches short because one-third of the audience can't see, one-third can't hear, and one-third are trying to locate a seat so that they will not drop their handbag, glass or plate, when they clap you.

Even if you decide to dispense with speeches altogether, you may find that after the cake is cut the crowd of well-wishers start chanting: 'Speech! Speech!', so that at least the bridegroom has to give a speech. Somebody will then decide to give an impromptu reply if the best man doesn't, which makes him feel he should have spoken. So if you are the best man, why not prepare a few words? You might then find that, having gone to the trouble of preparing a good speech and a joke just in case, you decide that you might as well give the speech anyway! See also pages 27–28 for advice on impromptu speeches.

Language barriers

If the bridegroom speaks little or no English, either he, or the bride and the family, may feel he ought to have the opportunity to speak at his own wedding, or that he has a duty to honour his hosts by thanking them publicly. There are two solutions. Either he speaks in his own language and an interpreter delivers a translation; the translator can be the bride or another person. Or he can remain silent except for nodding, smiling and lifting his glass, allowing the bride to speak on their behalf, making reference to him – 'my husband has asked me', etc. See pages 14–15 for more advice on planning your speech for a foreign audience.

After the party

When the party is over, members of the bridal party, and guests, should approach the speakers and thank them, complimenting them on a good speech. The bride and bridegroom, or hosts, could also express thanks in the form of a short note and accompanying photo or small gift.

Following the honeymoon, a party is often held to show the family photos of the trip. At the same time if a video has been taken of the wedding the speakers will want to see themselves. If they made any mistakes they will laugh and learn how they can improve, and if their performance was perfect they will be absolutely delighted.

chapter 4

Wedding Speeches

The following sample speeches are to suit different situations and speakers. Choose the most appropriate speech and substitute your own details. Alternatively, pick up a pen and a piece of paper and compose your own speech immediately after reading all these for inspiration.

The order of the speeches

The traditional order of toasts has a certain logic. The first speech leads up to a toast to the bride and bridegroom, the most important people. In effect, at a traditional wedding they are the honoured guests of the hosts, her parents. But while, as host, her father can talk about his new son-in-law, it would be a bit immodest for him to sing the praises of his daughter, so often a friend of the family is asked to speak and toast the couple, particularly if the father is going to speak later.

It falls to the bridegroom to reply to the first speech on behalf of himself and his bride. Whom should he thank? Both his in-laws, especially if they've paid for or organized the wedding, and especially his mother-in-law. Who else has helped? Presumably the bridesmaids. So he ends with a toast to the bridesmaids and/or Matron of Honour. If there are no bridesmaids the bridegroom can toast his bride, who can speak next in reply.

It is becoming more usual for the bride to speak at her wedding, either instead of her husband or as well as him. She can propose a toast to the bridegroom if the first toast was to her alone, or to the bridesmaids or Matron of

Honour. Alternatively, she can toast the family of the bridegroom, or if they are not present, the guests.

The best man then replies on behalf of the helpers (the bridesmaids). If there are no bridesmaids he does not have to speak, though he may wish to do so. The best man or the bridegroom can end his speech with a toast to the hosts, and the bride's father or mother, or both, can reply.

An optional final toast to HM The Queen is made at most Jewish weddings in the UK. Lastly, the best man or the toastmaster reads the telegrams in full if there are only a few, or reads the wittiest in full and then gives just the names of the senders of the others if there are many.

Variations to these customs can be made when there are no bridesmaids, or parents, or for a second marriage where the couple are paying for their own wedding.

When you have decided who is speaking, tell them all how many speakers there are and in which order they are speaking. Also check whom they will be toasting. And, of course, let them all know as soon as possible so that they have plenty of time to prepare.

How to give a toast
At the end of your speech, lift your glass in the air and then wait for everybody to stand and raise their glasses. Once all noise has finished, you can then give the toast.

Wedding speeches

The first speech: a toast to the bride and bridegroom
Brief toast at an informal wedding party:
'I would like to propose a toast to Annabelle and Steven, wishing them much joy and happiness for their future together. [Pause]
To Annabelle and Steven!'

Brief, simple, direct speech for the bride's father:
'Reverend Brown, Ladies and Gentlemen, all my guests [pause], I cannot tell you how pleased I am to see my daughter Annabelle looking so happy, as she begins life as Steven's wife. My wife and I do not feel that we are losing Annabelle, but entrusting her to Steven's good care. As we have got to know him, he has shown himself to be exactly the sort of person we hoped Annabelle would marry – charming, sincere, reliable – with a clear idea of what he wants from life and how to achieve it. I know that his many friends and family, as well as those who have only recently met him, think that this must be one of those marriages that are made in heaven, and will want to join me in wishing Steven and Annabelle a long and happy married life together. So please stand and raise your glasses, and drink to the health and happiness of Annabelle and Steven. [Pause]
To Annabelle and Steven!'

Longer, personalized speech by an old friend or relative when bride's father is present, but not making a speech:
'Annabelle's parents have done me the honour of offering me the opportunity to make a speech on this wonderful

occasion and propose a toast to Annabelle and Steven. When I asked why they chose me, George said: 'Because you are the President of the Oxford Drama Club [my bank manager/my oldest friend/the boss/have known us 25 years/the tallest/have the loudest voice]', and Martha said: 'Because you have known Annabelle since she was fourteen [a baby/a child/all her life/at school/at college/ you tell the best jokes].'

I have seen Annabelle acting [in school plays/at the drama club] on many occasions, and today she has a starring role. Over the years I have seen her develop many talents and accomplishments. She has won prizes for [drama/music/ essay-writing/cookery/coming top of her class in school], been awarded the first grade in [drama/music], studied [whatever is appropriate], learned how to [drive/ski/sail/ swim/dance/surf] and followed her interests in [whatever is appropriate], as well as finding time to [raise money for charity/do voluntary work with handicapped children/ attend church functions regularly/design clothes/paint/ draw] and help in her family's [shop/business/restaurant].

It was while she was at [school/college/work], that she met Steven who was [studying/working/travelling]. Though he had not yet [qualified as a doctor/passed his 'A' levels/ learnt to tell the difference between a gasket and a sprocket], it was obvious that they had much in common.

[Or: 'At first it didn't look as if they had much in common. But as they got to know each other Annabelle discovered that Steven liked [the arts as much as the sciences/hiking

as well as driving/driving cars as well as repairing them].
And Steven learned that Annabelle could [pilot a
plane/ice a cake/run a playgroup/speak fluent French].
And when Steven learned that [Annabelle/Annabelle's
father/mother/brother] was [an MP/barrister/Arsenal
supporter/had an amazing collection of Beatles records],
that clinched it.']

These young people have a bright future ahead of them, a
wonderful [career/job/home] planned in London [New
York/Sydney]. And I am sure you will want to join me in
wishing them every success and happiness in their new
venture and marriage. Please raise your glasses and drink
to the health and prosperity of Annabelle and Steven.
[Pause]
To Annabelle and Steven!'

Speech by relative/friend when the bride's father is recently deceased:

'It is my great pleasure to be here with you today on
this happy occasion and to help Annabelle and Steven
celebrate their marriage. I have known Annabelle and her
parents for many years, since [I/we/they] came to live in
[name of city].

Annabelle's late father, George, used to enjoy [a game of
football/a game of golf/fixing the car on Saturday after-
noons], and we spent many happy hours together
[sailing/relaxing] often accompanied by Steven. I remember George saying that Steven seemed to be a very [pleas-
ant/good-natured/hard-working/ambitious/talented]
young man. They got on well and George would have been

delighted to have seen this happy day. Although we miss George's presence, and his unfailing good humour, we know that he was looking forward to this wedding and we have fulfilled his hopes and wishes, and in a sense he is with us here today in our memories of him.

He would have been very satisfied to know what a comfort Steven has been to our family, how understanding, how supportive a friend in time of need, a valuable help to us in everything from fixing the car, taking over day to day decisions affecting [the business/work/ Annabelle's job], to just being there when we wanted advice and assistance. The wedding was postponed, but Annabelle is a girl well worth waiting for. Doesn't she look a picture today? George would have been proud of her, as I am sure Steven is. And it is with every confidence that I tell you I am sure that this young couple will have a very happy marriage, and I ask you to join me in wishing them both a long, happy and prosperous future together. Please stand and lift your glasses. I propose a toast – to Annabelle and Steven. [Pause]
To Annabelle and Steven!'

Speech suitable for an older man addressing a large, distinguished audience:

'Ladies and Gentlemen [pause], it is always a pleasure to attend a wedding. They say that the world loves a lover and I think this is true. Marriage is the expression of love, and also the start of a lifelong adventure. Plato said: 'The beginning is the most important part of the work.' If that is the case, then Annabelle and Steven have been lucky in enjoying the most wonderful beginning. They already have most of the good gifts one would wish upon a young couple. Annabelle is a beautiful bride, Steven is a handsome husband, and both come from secure family homes where their parents have set examples of what a good marriage should be.

A good marriage is not something you can create on your own without help from your partner. It is a joint venture. Marriage is like a journey in a boat. You cannot drill a hole in the boat and when water floods in say to your companion: 'It's nothing to do with me, the water is coming in on your side of the boat.' You must row in the same direction. In fact, love has been defined as not looking at each other, but looking in the same direction.

If marriage is a boat, then many of us are in the same boat! Annabelle and Steven, you are embarking on a wonderful journey, and you have many friends who will support you, and help you, and wish you well. I would now like to ask everyone in this room to stand with me, and raise their glasses. I propose a toast to the long life, health, wealth and happy marriage of Annabelle and Steven. [Pause]
To Annabelle and Steven!'

Best man's toast to bride and bridegroom
Impromptu speech at a very small wedding without bridesmaids:
'This is a lovely small, intimate gathering of friends, which is the way Annabelle and Steven wanted it to be. And we all appreciate how honoured we are to be among the select few who they have chosen to share this special

occasion with them. Everyone here is a close friend or relative and we all have personal knowledge of Annabelle's unique qualities, her kindness, her gift for creating a happy atmosphere and her loyal friendship. And we are delighted that she is marrying Steven, who is so [loved/admired] by his family and close friends and is respected by all of us for his [hard work/talents/skills/zest for life]. He shares many of her good qualities and they both deserve all the good things in life. So let's wish them both a very happy married life together. Has everyone got a drink? Good. [Pause]

To Annabelle and Steven.'

An alternative could be:

'It gives me special pleasure to be present at the wedding of my good friends Annabelle and Steven, because I introduced them at [name of the venue] and because I have known both of them for many years at [school/the tennis club]. May their lives continue with equal joy and may they share many happy occasions and reunions such as this with our families and friends. Here's to Annabelle and Steven. [Pause]

To Annabelle and Steven.'

Toast to the bride's parents

Bridegroom's speech, replying to first toast to bride and bridegroom. A longer, humorous speech:

'Reverend Brown, Ladies and Gentlemen [pause], thank you very much, George, for those kind words. It goes almost without saying how pleased I am to be here today. In order not to dull your pleasure I intend to speak for only a few minutes in case we all [get snowed in/melt away in the heat]! We couldn't have wished for better weather – [perfect sunshine, just the right start for a marriage/a beautiful, romantic white Christmas].

Annabelle is beautiful, intelligent and hard-working. The list of her good qualities is extremely long, although unfortunately I cannot read her handwriting. As you all know, Annabelle has been a much sought-after girl, but I'm pleased to announce the winner of the competition – me. There are no runners up, or associated prizes.

My new mother-in-law, Martha, has worked long and hard for many months to prepare this wonderful occasion, all the little details such as these beautiful [flowers/cake decorations] were planned by her, and my father-in-law has taken on his second mortgage without complaint, like the good-natured man he is. I am very pleased to be part of their family and to know that my parents feel the same.

Speaking of whom, today represents a great occasion for both my parents, being the culmination of many years of planning of a different sort. They have prepared me well, supported me through university and taught me the difference between right and wrong, so that I know which I am enjoying at any given time!

I would like to thank you all for your presence – in both senses of the word, but especially for the smiling faces I see in front of me. I am particularly pleased that Aunt Alice managed to make the long journey down to Surrey from Aberdeen for this occasion, and we are all delighted that

Annabelle's sister, Louise, flew all the way from Australia to join us and be such a charming bridesmaid. Of course, she had a 'little help' – quite a big help, actually, from Tracey, who looked so sweet holding Annabelle's train.

My best man, Alan, has made everything go smoothly, and I appreciate his contribution to what has been a perfect day.

Finally, I must pay tribute to the bridesmaids Louise, Natalie, Margaret and Sue, whose invaluable support has helped to make this day so successful.'

If there are no bridesmaids, the toast is to his parents-in-law as follows:

'In conclusion, thank you, everybody, for listening, and I hope you are having a wonderful [afternoon/evening] and are all as happy as we are today. Would you kindly stand and raise your glasses and drink a toast to the health of your hosts, two wonderful people, George and Martha. [Pause]
To George and Martha!'

A brief but sincere speech:
'My wife and I [pause for laughter] thank you for your kind words. It is wonderful to be surrounded by so many friends and good wishes. We have been overwhelmed by the kindness and help we have received, the generous gifts, and the people who have made extra contributions on this, our special day. I must mention the bridesmaids who have done so much to help my wife, and added

glamour to the photographs that will remind us of this very happy occasion. [Pause]

To the bridesmaids!'

Toast to bridegroom and both families
Informal toast by the bride:

'I'd like to propose a toast to the most wonderful man in the world, my new husband Steven. I'd also like to thank his parents for what they have contributed over the years to make him the person he is, supporting him through college, and also for making me such a welcome member of their family. I must also thank my parents for everything they have done for me and especially this wonderful event, my wedding to Steven. May we all meet on many more happy occasions. [Pause]

To Steven.'

Toast to the groom's parents
Reply by the bride's father to the bridegroom's toast, giving personal family marriage details:

'Thank you, Steven. As you know Annabelle is our only daughter so this will be our only chance to stage what has been a lovely wedding. And we did not want to miss the opportunity of having such a wonderful day, complete with the white wedding car. When my parents' generation were marrying back in the Second World War, wedding couples needed clothing coupons from all their relatives to make the wedding dress and wedding suits, all of which had to be of sensible material so that they could be worn again. Everybody saved all their food coupons for the wedding cake. Since you could not go abroad, you honeymooned on the south coast at resorts such as

Bournemouth where there was barbed wire on the beaches. For each generation the circumstances are different. Today, guests have flown in from [Australia/ America/France] to be with Annabelle and Steven – something that would have been very rare sixty years ago. We have a photographer visiting us to make a video, so that we can remember this magical day for the rest of our lives, and all the wedding photos will be able to be digitally altered to hide my bald patch!

We want Annabelle and Steven to enjoy the things we never had, not to take them for granted, but to appreciate how lucky they are to be able to celebrate like this, surrounded by their families and friends.

I know that Steven's parents understand how glad we are to do whatever we can for our daughter, and their son. We are very pleased to have Gregory and Gillian and their family here to celebrate with us. Their generous support and presence, joining in enthusiastically with everything we planned, has enabled us to truly enjoy this day. So please join me in drinking a toast to the health of my son-in-law's parents, Gregory and Gillian. [Pause]
To Gregory and Gillian.'

Second weddings

Today, second weddings are increasingly common (around 40% of people marrying in the UK have firsthand experience of the proceedings), but it is important to remember that it is still a special occasion for all involved and may indeed be a first wedding for one of the partners. Try to be upbeat and positive in your speech and avoid too much talk of the couple's past or marital history. Don't dwell, even in jest, on the fact that the first marriage did not work. It may be appropriate to pay tribute to a former or ex-wife or husband. Perhaps he or she sadly died. Make sure you check this first with a close family member. Don't spring unknowns on the bride and bridegroom or their entourage. Be tactful, sensitive and discreet.

Your role is not to highlight that this is a second union, but to welcome all present, to embrace and bring together all the guests and family members in order to celebrate the special event. The strategy is inclusion not exclusion. There may be some fragile or delicately balanced relationships between families and individuals among those assembled – your role is to bridge any chasms, not highlight any gulfs. Don't tread on anyone's toes or you will want to hotfoot it out of there. And if there are children from either or both sides, make sure you include them in the toast, having checked with the bride or bridegroom about any sensitive areas.

Toasts to bride and bridegroom at a second wedding
Speech by best man at a second wedding:

'I think I speak for everyone in this room when I say how happy I am to see Stephen and Mary married – at last. And I say 'at last' because this is a second marriage for both of them, and they truly deserve this and every future moment of happiness. Every wedding is special, but this one is doubly so. Stephen and Mary were tailor-made for each other – a perfect match, as we can all see today. Both are courageous (as today's second foray into the conjugal jungle proves!), they complement each other, in both senses of the word, and they are committed, compassionate and caring (all the 'c' words men usually avoid!). Not only did they embrace each other, but they also embraced each other's children, relatives, friends, hopes, fears and dreams. We are celebrating not only the union of two lovely people, but also of two families, two lives and two futures. And it would not have been such a wonderful day without the beautiful bridesmaids and page boys [toast by name] and the wonderful hard work and organization by all those responsible [toast by name]. Let's raise our glasses now to the beautiful, blissful bride and the gorgeous groom with the biggest grin in the world. Ladies and gentlemen, please charge your glasses. [Pause]

I give you Stephen and Mary.

Short, happy, slightly humorous speech for a bride enjoying her first marriage to a divorced man:

'Annabelle, for you this is a first marriage and a time of excitement and hope. For Steven it is a second marriage. He liked marriage so much that despite all the difficulties of his first attempt, when he met you he decided to try it again. Annabelle, you may not realize it, but you are gaining the advantage of marrying a man who has had the sharp corners rubbed off him. A mature specimen. A vintage blend.

We hope that you will always enjoy life together, a very long and happy life together, and that you will always retain the enthusiasm of this new start, and remember the joy and delight of finding each other, which is so evident today. So we will all raise our glasses to you and toast your future. [Pause]
To Annabelle and Steven.'

Short, happy, slightly humorous speech when the bridegroom is marrying for the first time, to a divorced woman:
'Steven, for you this is a first marriage and a time of expectation and hope. For Annabelle it is a second marriage. You must be especially proud today, because she liked you so much that despite all the difficulties of her first marriage, when she met you she decided to try it again. What an honour!

Annabelle, you have the advantage of experience. Steven, you are gaining many advantages by marrying a mature woman. We hope that both of you will always enjoy married life, a very long and happy life together. And that you will always retain the enthusiasm of this new start and remember the joy and delight of finding each other, which is so evident today. So we will all raise our glasses to you and toast your future. [Pause]
To Annabelle and Steven.'

Sincere speech by a friend at a second or third marriage where both parties have been divorced or widowed at least once.
(Select part, or all, of the following paragraphs, according to whether the parties have been recently widowed/divorced or alone for many years.)

'All marriages are special occasions, but a second marriage is a doubly precious time because you do not take everything for granted. You realize how very lucky you are to be given another chance to be happy, and appreciate the blessing you have received in finding a soulmate and companion you can trust. It is a time of renewed hope.

I know that the two of you who are getting married today feel it is wonderful to be with so many good friends, and in particular one good friend, who understands your heartaches as well as your joys. That is so important.

It is a pleasure for you to experience an end to loneliness and sadness, and a joy for us to be witnesses and share this beginning with you. When you have experienced past disappointments, hardship and disillusionment, you know you have been up and down on life's waves. And when you are in the troughs of those waves, you sometimes wonder when you will ever come up again. Yet there is always a chance anew, an opportunity to feel love for someone, just like the first time. The past does not burden the present – but you learn by it, and do not repeat your mistakes. You have an opportunity through experience for knowing better than anyone else what is at stake and how much effort it takes, and what a loss it is if you don't do everything you can to make your partner contented. How fortunate you are to have found yet another chance at happiness together, with a better understanding than most people of what you should do to make a successful marriage, and how much you will gain.

It is difficult late in life to put away the past, and start again, but you have all the means at your disposal to make a success of the venture. Everyone has the right to happiness, and should you have the chance to find happiness, whether you are someone young starting life again, or a grandmother, why not?

We are confident that you will now receive the joy you deserve, and we are really happy for you. I speak for everyone here when I say we wish you all the best, and hope that for you [pause] 'the best is yet to come'. So, Annabelle and Steven, we would like to drink a toast to your happy future together. [Pause]
To Annabelle and Steven.'

Same-sex marriages

Laws about same-sex marriages vary from place to place and change constantly. Same-sex unions are becoming more common, and you may find yourself invited to attend or speak at such an occasion in the future. You will have been chosen to speak because you are an understanding and sympathetic person who knows the couple well. It will be important to do your research about the guest list, the age range involved, any strong feelings or possible hostility and what the couple feel might not be appropriate or what they would particularly like you to say. Ask yourself a few questions about your speech before you run it past the couple, in order to ensure that it is not potentially offensive, negative or ambivalent. Make it a positive and inclusive speech, celebrating the occasion, bridging any differences there may be in the audience and embracing diversity. Speak from the heart, be straightforward, genuine and open-minded. Address everyone in the room, ensuring that each guest feels an important part of the celebration. Remember that this may well be the first gay or lesbian ceremony that some of the guests have attended.

Speech to the couple by the best man:
'Firstly, I would like to welcome every one of you here to this very special occasion. We are all celebrating a wonderful day, when John and Simon have been able to pledge their love and commitment to each other in a formal context and in front of all those whom they love and are loved by. I wanted to give them a big round of applause during the ceremony, but why don't we do just that here and now!

Today is a significant occasion not only for John and Simon, but also for their families and friends, all of whom were able to witness and share in their joy. It is a day when we celebrate diversity and tolerance, when we embrace and rejoice in individual choice, a day when we come together united by the same thoughts and hopes – that John and Simon enjoy a future filled with deep joy, good health and true friendship. They have brought happiness to their friends and it is a pleasure to be able to return some of that today. Please join me in wishing them both a wonderful life together and pledging our commitment to them as their friends and family. [Pause] To John and Simon!'

Reply by couple:
'Thank you, David, for such a wonderful, eloquent speech. Thank you for being our best man and for supporting us throughout our preparations for today, and for not forgetting the rings! Simon and I feel honoured to be surrounded by so many close friends and family, all of whom have wished us well on our wedding day and embraced our decision to be together with such generosity of spirit and tolerance. Most of all, I would like to thank our parents for everything they have done. Reaching this point was a challenge for us and for them, but with their help, support, love and concern and that of all our friends and relatives, we were able to fulfil our greatest wish and be formally united. Embracing the new is not always easy. But life is full of change and developments, without which we would move backwards instead of forwards as a society. So let's toast the future – ours and yours. To you, from us – all the joy in the world.'

Wedding speeches to avoid

Regardless of the specific nature of the occasion, there are certain things that you should always avoid saying when asked to give a speech at a wedding. Some of these are as follows:

Over-apologetic speech:

'I don't know why anyone picked me to give a speech. I've never given a speech in my life before. I'm sure you don't want a long speech, but I've tried to prepare something, and I hope it's all right. Anyway, I did make some notes somewhere [silence]. Well, I can't find them, but [pause], oh, here it is. I've got a joke! 'As I was on my way to the wedding' [pause]. Oh, I've dropped it! Can you move your chair? No, don't bother. It's not really funny and you've probably heard it anyway. Most of you don't know Alf, but I expect you'll want to wish him, and the bride of course, a happy, er, future.'

Negative speech – and rather too revealing!

'I don't like speeches and I didn't want to give a speech, but Martha insisted I should. I suppose there was nobody else. I'm not a good speaker so I'm not going to bore you by making a long speech. Annabelle's a nice girl. I went out with her for a long time before she decided to marry Steven, or he decided to marry her. So I suppose it's what she wanted and she's done the right thing. Anyway, they know each other pretty well, having been living together for two years now. They wouldn't have got married if she hadn't been pregnant, so the baby has done something good. I know her Mum's pleased. The baby's going to be a big change. Everyone says: 'May all your troubles be little ones.' Apart from that I don't suppose they'll have any troubles. Marriage won't be a big change for them as they'll be living in the same place, you know. So everything is going to be all right, more or less.

Er – what else am I supposed to say? If you haven't got a drink the bar's still open. Prices are a bit steep, but you don't go to weddings every day. We're going to pass the hat round later, buy some beer and go back to their place. Annabelle's shaking her head. What's the matter? Don't you want us to? Steve says it's all right. Anyway, if you can't afford the whisky and you haven't got any beer left, grab a glass of water. To Annabelle and Steven! Can I sit down now?'

Extremely brief reply from the bridegroom:
'Thank you.'

Depressing speech:
'Relatives and friends, the one person missing here today is, of course, Annabelle's father, and no day can be really happy without him with us. Though I have tried to take his place, it is mere formality. No-one can take his place. Our happiness would have been complete if he had been here. Alas, he is not. We miss his help and his advice, as a husband to Martha, and father to Annabelle. He made so many plans for this wedding. If only he could have seen Annabelle today … [breaks off]. Has somebody got a handkerchief to give to Annabelle?'

Reluctant father-in-law's speech:
'We're very pleased to see Annabelle getting married, at last. When I first met Steven I didn't like him very much, because of his hair and his clothes and the fact that he didn't have a steady job, but now I've got to know him he doesn't seem too bad. All these are things that can be changed. I'm sure Annabelle could change him if she wanted to, but she seems to like him the way he is. We're sorry that his Mum, what's her name?, died, and that his Dad didn't come along with his new stepmother, but perhaps it's just as well. Anyway, um, where was I? Well, er, I think that's everything. Let's all have a drink. Was I supposed to toast somebody?'

Gushing speech:
'I am deeply honoured to be invited to this momentous and lavish occasion by my esteemed friends, Martha and George. It is a privilege to pay them this small token of respect. I am sure Martha will forgive me for saying that her very presence excites envy from others. Martha has always been admired for her brilliant elegance, the epitome of good taste. The evidence before our eyes is her faultless attention to detail in these exquisite flower decorations. It has been a day that commenced so stunningly with the horse and carriage procession, swept forward with the harmonious, soaring, musical arrangements at the wedding ceremony, and has culminated in the utter perfection of the gourmet dinner, all in keeping with what we have come to expect from the organizational abilities of one of the world's paragons. No woman on earth could have been a more devoted, exacting, wife and mother, and Annabelle has admirably followed her mother's fine

example, having inherited flawless cover-girl looks, and demonstrating impeccable good manners. You will, I am quite sure, agree with me totally when I say, our beautiful, delectable Annabelle is irreplaceable, and we shall miss her dreadfully, when she departs across the skies to the beautiful tropical paradise that she will enhance immeasurably.'

Long pompous speech:
'Your Royal Highness, Ladies and Gentlemen, as a minister, judge and professor, I feel I am in a good position to speak about the history of marriage, its importance in society, and the duties of the married couple to each other and the wider community. First, the history of marriage [continues]…

Now, we shall continue with the sayings of the numerous venerable sages [continues]…

Well, I agreed not to speak for more than half an hour, but I see that I have been speaking for a little longer than forty-five minutes. I could continue considerably longer on this fascinating subject, in fact I have several pages of notes here if anybody wishes to come and ask me any questions. Unfortunately I am obliged to terminate at this stage, because someone has just passed me a note saying that the band has to depart at 11pm and it is now 10.30. So I will conclude by saying that [continues]…'

chapter 5

Readings at Weddings

Some people feel awkward about expressing their feelings in public, but readings and poems are an ideal way to get around this problem, as well as adding variation, depth and interest.

Inevitably, older texts sound more formal but their beauty and elegance can enhance even the most informal of ceremonies, adding a note of dignity and seriousness, and emphasizing the importance of the occasion.

During the ceremony

Although it is a matter of personal choice as to when the texts are read, the following would generally be considered appropriate during the marriage ceremony itself.

**To express the depth of the bride
or bridegroom's love for their partner:
Sonnets from the Portuguese 43**
Elizabeth Barrett Browning (1806–61)

How do I love thee? Let me count the ways.
I love thee to the depth and breadth and height
My soul can reach, when feeling out of sight
For the ends of being and ideal grace.
I love thee to the level of everyday's
Most quiet need, by sun and candlelight.
I love thee freely, as men strive for right;
I love thee purely, as they turn from praise.
I love thee with the passion put to use
In my old griefs, and with my childhood's faith.

I love thee with a love I seemed to lose
With my lost saints – I love thee with the breath,
Smiles, tears, of all my life! – and, if God choose,
I shall but love thee better after death.

To emphasize that two is better than one:
Love's Philosophy
Percy Bysshe Shelley (1792–1822)

The fountains mingle with the river
And the rivers with the oceans,
The winds of heaven mix forever
With a sweet emotion;
Nothing in the world is single,
All things by a law divine
In one another's being mingle –
Why not I with thine?

See the mountain's kiss high heaven
And the waves clasp one another;
No sister-flower would be forgiven
If it disdain'd its brother:

And the sunlight clasps the earth,
And the moonbeams kiss the sea –
What are all these kissings worth,
If thou kiss not me?

**To express how important the bride's
happiness is to the groom:**
The Passionate Shepherd to His Love
Christopher Marlowe (1564–93)

Come live with me and be my love,
And we will all the pleasures prove
That hills and valleys, dales and fields
And all the craggy mountains yields.
There we will sit upon the rocks,
Seeing the shepherds feed their flocks
By shallow rivers, to whose falls
Melodious birds sing madrigals.
And I will make thee beds of roses
With a thousand fragrant posies,
A cap of flowers and a kirtle
Embroidered all with leaves of myrtle;

A gown made of the finest wool,
Which from our pretty lambs we pull;
Fair lined slippers for the cold,
With buckles of the purest gold;

A belt of straw and ivy buds,
With coral-clasps and amber studs;
And if these pleasures may thee move,
Come live with me and be my love.
The shepherd swains shall dance and sing
For thy delight each May morning;
If these delights thy mind may move,
Then live with me, and be my love.

To emphasize the strength of their love:
From The Sonnets
William Shakespeare (1564–1616)

Shall I compare thee to a summer's day?
Thou art more lovely and more temperate:
Rough winds do shake the darling buds of May,
And summer's lease hath all too short a date:
Sometime too hot the eye of heaven shines,
And often is his gold complexion dimmed;
And every fair from fair sometime declines,
By chance or nature's changing course untrimmed;
But thy eternal summer shall not fade,
Nor lose possession of that fair thou owest;
Nor shall death brag thou wander'st in his shade,
When in eternal lines to time thou growest:
So long as men can breathe, or eyes can see,
So long lives this, and this gives life to thee.

Let me not to the marriage of true minds
Admit impediments. Love is not love
Which alters when it alteration finds,
Or bends with the remover to remove:
O, no! it is an ever-fixed mark,
That looks on tempests and is never shaken;
It is the star to every wandering barque,
Whose worth's unknown, although his height be taken.
Love's not time's fool, though rosy lips and cheeks
Within his bending sickle's compass come;
Love alters not with his brief hours and weeks,
But bears it out even to the edge of doom.
If this be error and upon me proved,
I never writ, nor no man ever loved.

On the nature of love:
From The Prophet, on love
Kahlil Gibran (1883–1931)

Love has no other desire but to fulfil itself.
But if you love and must needs have desires, let these
  be your desires:
To melt and be like a running brook that sings its
  melody to the night.
To know the pain of too much tenderness.
To be wounded by your own understanding of love;
And to bleed willingly and joyfully.
To wake at dawn with a winged heart and give thanks
  for another day of loving;
To rest at the noon hour and meditate love's ecstacy;
To return home at eventide with gratitude;
And then to sleep with a prayer for the beloved in your
  heart and a song of praise on your lips.

**On the strength that comes from understanding
between a couple and the partnership of marriage:**
I Ching, The Book of Changes

But when two people are at one in their innermost
  hearts,
They shatter even the strength of iron or bronze.
And when two people understand each other in their
  innermost hearts,
Their words are sweet and strong, like the fragrance of
  orchids.

To express their happiness and love for each other:
To My Dear And Loving Husband
Anne Bradstreet (c.1612–72)

If ever two were one, then surely we.
If ever man were loved by wife, then thee;
If ever wife was happy in a man,
Compare with me, ye woman, if you can.
I prize thy love more than whole mines of gold
Or all the riches that the East doth hold.
My love is such that rivers cannot quench,
Nor ought but love from thee, give recompense.
Thy love is such I can no way repay,
The heavens reward thee manifold, I pray.
The while we live, in love let's so persevere,
That when we live no more, we may live ever.

On how love and friendship go hand in hand:
This Day I Married My Best Friend
Author unknown

This day I married my best friend
The one I laugh with as we share life's wondrous zest,
As we find new enjoyments and experience all that's best.
The one I live for because the world seems brighter
As our happy times are better and our burdens feel
    much lighter.
The one I love with every fibre of my soul.
We used to feel vaguely incomplete, now together we
    are whole.

Offering advice to the couple:
From Marriage Advice
Jane Wells (c. 1886)

Never go to bed angry.

Let your love be stronger than your hate or anger.

Learn the wisdom of compromise, for it is better to bend a little than to break.

Believe the best rather than the worst.

People have a way of living up or down to your opinion of them.

Remember that true friendship is the basis for any lasting relationship.

The person you choose to marry is deserving of the courtesies and kindnesses you bestow on your friends.

On the future
The Blessing Of The Apaches
Author unknown

Now you will feel no rain,

For each of you will be shelter to the other.

Now you will feel no cold,

For each of you will be warmth to the other.

Now there is no more loneliness for you,

For each of you will be companion to the other.

Now you are two bodies,

But there is only one life before you.

May beauty surround you both in the journey ahead and through all the years.

May happiness be your companion and your days be good and long upon the earth.

On the nature of marriage:
From The Prophet, on marriage
Kahlil Gibran (1883–1931)

Then Almitra spoke again and said, 'And what of
  Marriage, master?'
And he answered saying:
You were born together, and together you shall be
  forevermore.
You shall be together when white wings of death scatter
  your days.
Aye, you shall be together even in the silent memory of
  God.
But let there be spaces in your togetherness,
And let the winds of the heavens dance between you.
Love one another but make not a bond of love:
Let it rather be a moving sea between the shores of your
  souls.
Fill each other's cup but drink not from one cup.
Give one another of your bread but eat not from the
  same loaf.
Sing and dance together and be joyous, but let each one
  of you be alone,
Even as the strings of a lute are alone though they
  quiver with the same music.

Give your hearts, but not into each other's keeping.
For only the hand of Life can contain your hearts.
And stand together, yet not too near together:
For the pillars of the temple stand apart,
And the oak tree and the cypress grow not in each
  other's shadow.

On love:
Corinthians 13:4–8, The Bible
Love is patient and kind; love is not jealous or boastful; it is not arrogant or rude. Love does not insist on its own way; it is not irritable or resentful; it does not rejoice at wrong, but rejoices in the right. Love bears all things, believes all things, hopes all things, endures all things. Love never ends.

Humorous readings

The following texts are more light-hearted or humorous and so are ideal for including in the speeches at the reception.

Bride to the bridegroom
Yes, I'll Marry You
Pam Ayres [1947–]

Yes, I'll marry you, my dear,
And here's the reason why;
So I can push you out of bed
When the baby starts to cry.

To Keep Your Marriage Brimming
Ogden Nash (1902–71)

To keep your marriage brimming,
With love in the loving cup,
Whenever you're wrong admit it;
Whenever you're right shut up.

Best man or bridegroom on the woman's role in marriage:
Wedding Song
Traditional verse

Now some people think it's jolly for to lead a single life,
But I believe in marriage and the comforts of a wife.
In fact, you might have quarrels, just an odd one now and
    then,
It's worth your while a-falling out to make it up again.
> *[Chorus] Get a little table, then a little chair,*
> *And then a little house in the corner of a square,*
> *Get a little teapot and save a little tin,*
> *But don't forget the cradle for to rock the baby in.*

A married man has comforts where a single man has not,
His clothes is always mended and his meals is always hot.
No matter what your trouble is your wife'll pull you through,
So if you think of marriage, lads, I'll tell you what to do.
> *[Chorus]*

A single man in lodgings can't have much delight,
For there's no-one to speak to when he sits home at night,
Nothing to attract him or to pass his time away,
So he'll quickly find the difference if he listens what I say.
> *[Chorus]*

It's little use of asking a girl to marry you,
Unless you've got a little corner of the table too,
For a good wife loves to see you cosy, clean and nice,
So if you wish to marry, boys, I'll tell you what to do.
> *[Chorus]*

.gh any family member could read this 'recipe', or ꞏ en the best man, it would be perfect for the mother of the bride. It could also be adapted to suit the couple, such as 2 kilos of DIY, 500 grams of mowing the lawn, 750 grams of delicious home cooking, etc.

A Good Wedding Cake
Author unknown

4lb of love.
1lb butter of youth.
½lb of good looks.
1lb sweet temper.
1lb of blindness of faults.
1lb of self forgetfulness.
1lb of pounded wit.
1lb of good humour.
2 tablespoons of sweet argument.
1 pint of rippling laughter.
1 wine glass of common sense.
1oz of modesty.

Put the love, good looks and sweet temper into a well furnished house. Beat the butter of youth to a cream, and mix well together with the blindness of faults. Stir the pounded wit and good humour into the sweet argument, then add the rippling laughter and common sense. Work the whole together until everything is well mixed, and bake gently for ever.

chapter 6

Jokes & Quotes

This chapter will provide you with some of the content, reference material or raw materials for your speeches in the form of jokes, quotes, stories and anecdotes. Regardless of which you choose, it is vital that it is used properly and not just peppered into your speech. The following framework may help:

Item–Point–Relevance

Item: When using 'item–point–relevance', first we use the item, i.e. we tell the joke, recount the story or anecdote, show the picture or quote the quote.

Point: Often speakers are guilty of using quotes, humour stories, etc. without explaining why they are using them. For example, if a father was telling a story about his daughter's persistence in life in a father-of-the-bride speech it can often help to complete the circle by explaining the point of the story.

Relevance: Having told the story and/or explained the point, it may be necessary then to explain the relevance of that point within the overall context of the speech or to the audience who are listening to the speech.

Here's an example:

Item
'Carl Jung said: 'The meeting of two personalities is like the contact of two chemical substances; if there is any reaction, both are transformed.' '

Point
'I believe the point that Jung was making was that when two people meet and connect, who they are changes forever as a result of that meeting.'

Relevance
'And when Chris and Sue met there was a reaction and both have been transformed forever. This fantastic transformation has managed to bring out the best in both of them as they are blooming with happiness, confidence and kindness.'

When using item–point–relevance, it is key that its use is not too structured and rigid and avoids the direct use of the three words. When used effectively this completes the circle of a good story by ensuring that the point you are making is clearly understood and the audience can see how it relates to your speech and the occasion overall.

Jokes and humour

Jokes and humour can also sometimes add to the interest and quality of your speeches. However, before embarking on using them you should apply the pre-joke checklist to avoid coming badly unstuck:

- Are you funny/good at telling jokes? Beware of the difference between perception and reality. Just because you've been told you are a funny guy does not mean you are a good joke teller. Get some feedback from a neutral, direct and candid person. If the answer's not a firm and immediate 'yes', then leave it out. For those of us that are not fantastic joke tellers, personal anecdotes or stories are often a far more appropriate solution.

- Is this joke appropriate for the audience? Sex, politics and religion are all sensitive subjects. This is not to say that jokes about them should never be used. The point is, is the joke appropriate for this audience? If in any doubt, take a representative member of the audience to one side and ask them for some honest feedback.

- Is this the right moment of the speech for a joke? Humour has its place within speeches. It is often good as an engagement item near the beginning or during the main body. However, if you have spent time building up strong feelings and emotions in your audience by, for example, talking seriously about love at a wedding, you need to think carefully about then blowing this good work apart with a sledgehammer joke.

- Is the joke actually funny? (to this audience) You must dry-run jokes with typical audience members. Just because it had your friends in stitches does not mean it will have the same effect upon an older audience. Sometimes the humour just won't translate.

- Is the audience likely to have heard the joke before? Be careful about borrowing humour from the media as it could fall flat if everyone has heard it before.

Once you have ticked off this list, you then have licence to try to be funny, but how do you pull it off?

Entire books have been written on being funny and we won't attempt to replicate them here. Here are a few guidelines to jokes within speeches:

- Focus on how you tell the joke: As Frank Carson says: 'It's the way I tell 'em.' Good delivery of jokes is a prerequisite to telling them at all.

- Timing: Never, ever rush the punch line.

- Practise, practise and practise again: Just as with any rehearsal, knowing the joke inside out will free you up to focus on how you're delivering it.

- Make it personal: Substitute audience members' names for the names of the people in the joke.

- Concealed jokes: Try starting your joke in your normal speech style and audience members won't see it for what it is. Then when the light bulb comes on the impact is magnified.

Below are a short selection of jokes and amusing one-liners that might be appropriate for use at weddings.

A little girl went to a wedding. Afterwards, she asked her mother why the bride changed her mind. 'What do you mean?' responded her mother. 'Well, she went down the aisle with one man, and came back with another.'

I like the story of the woman who had an artist paint a portrait of her covered with jewels. Her explanation:

'If I die and my husband remarries, I want his next wife to go crazy looking for the jewels.'

In the first year of marriage, the man speaks and the woman listens. In the second year, the woman speaks and the man listens. In the third year, they both speak and the neighbours listen.

The other day I overheard a woman telling her friend,
'It is I who made my husband a millionaire.'
'And what was he before you married him?' asked the friend.
The woman replied, 'A multi-millionaire'.

A best man's speech should be like a mini-skirt: short enough to be interesting, but long enough to cover the bare essentials.

One day a man inserted an advert in the local classifieds: 'Wife wanted'.
The next day he received a hundred letters. They all said the same thing: 'You can have mine.'

Rules for finding a successful mate:
1 It is important to find a man who works around the house, occasionally cooks and cleans, and who has a job.
2 It is important to find a man who makes you laugh.
3 It is important to find a man who is dependable and doesn't lie.
4 It is important to find a man who worships your body.
5 It is vital that these four men never meet.

Stories and Anecdotes

As the saying goes, reality is often stranger, and funnier, than fiction. Whereas joke-telling relies to a certain extent on a degree of natural aptitude, most people are able to recount stories, either of events that have happened to them or to others. When combined with dynamic delivery, in terms of use of voice, facial expressions and body language, stories and anecdotes can be a lot funnier than jokes. An added advantage is that we find it a lot easier to recall and tell stories than we do to memorize and tell jokes, where we often trip over the punch line.

Although you can collect stories and anecdotes from reference books such as this, often the most effective ones are from your own experience. Ask yourself: 'What is the subject of this speech or presentation?' and then: 'What are some of my more memorable experiences with the subject of the speech?' These two simple questions will often unearth excellent and relevant stories. Here are some thought starters for personal stories about you and the bride/groom.

- Where did you meet?
- How long have you known them?
- Were you at school together?
- Have you ever been on holiday with them?
- Do you share any hobbies?
- How did they describe their husband/wife to you when they first met them?

Quotations

Quotations are another useful source of interesting content for speechmakers. They are effective since they can add impact and credibility to the point you are making, gain the audience's attention and sometimes make them laugh. Here are some key guidelines to help ensure that you use the right quote, at the right time, to the right audience:

Key guidelines:

- Don't use too many quotes: You will lessen their impact and your speech will become mechanical

- Limit them to one or two sentences: Audiences start switching off when they are read long quotes. Quotes are often most memorable when in a short, well-structured single sentence, e.g. 'I hear and I forget, I see and I remember, I do and I understand.'

- If you're not sure who said it, say so, but don't guess, or you risk undermining your speech. For example: 'Another form of reference material is statistics, but we must be careful with their use as we all recall the famous quote: 'There are three kinds of lies: lies, damned lies and statistics.' '

- Make sure they are relevant: Just because you like a quote or think it is funny doesn't mean to say it will add to the effectiveness of your speech, it may just leave the audience wondering why on earth you have used it.

- Unless you are a great actor or orator, avoid any verse over four lines long. Five-line limericks, however, add humour, but be sure they are in good taste. Seek them out in a good poetry anthology.

Libraries and bookshops will, of course, stock treasuries of quotations. Consider using quotes from well-known humorous writers such as James Thurber, Charles Dickens, Mark Twain or Oscar Wilde.

Songwriters are another good source of quotable lines. You can track down the words of songwriters from books or librettos or some CD sleeves. Good songwriters to quote include W.S. Gilbert, Sammy Cahn and Noel Coward. Alternatively, refer to a good dictionary of popular music.

American quotations can be found among the sayings of every president, while politics, business, morality and deter-mination to win against the odds are popular subjects.

Adapting quotations

The more you can relate your quotations to your audi-ence and your subject matter, the more interested they will be. If the only quotation you can find is not very relevant or complimentary, adapt it. For example, at the wedding of a soldier you could start: 'According to the British Grenadiers, 'Some talk of Alexander, and some of Hercules, and others of Lysander and such great names as these.' But I would rather talk about Captain (groom's name).'

Below is a short selection of quotations that you might find appropriate for your wedding speech.

Advice
Live within your means, even if you have to borrow money to do it. *Anonymous*

Age
Wrinkles should merely indicate where smiles have been. *Mark Twain, 19th century American author and humorist*

Count your age with friends but not with years. *Anonymous*

Anger
Every minute you spend being angry with your partner is a waste of sixty seconds in which you could be enjoying yourselves. *Anonymous*

Babies
A baby is an alimentary canal with a loud voice at one end and no responsibility at the other. *Ronald Reagan, 20th century American President*

There are two things in this life for which we are never fully prepared: twins. *John Billings, 19th century American humorist*

Bachelors
Advice for those about to marry. Don't. *Punch magazine, 1845*

Children
Anybody who hates children and dogs can't be all bad.
W.C. Fields, 20th century American actor and comedian

There is only one beautiful child in the world and every mother has it. *Stephen Leacock, 20th century Canadian author and humorist*

Families
Important families are like potatoes. The best parts are underground. *Francis Bacon, 20th century British artist*

Home
There is no place like home after the other places close.
Anonymous

Honesty
The best measurement of a man's honesty isn't his income tax return. It's the zero adjustment on his bathroom scales. *Arthur C. Clarke, 20th century English writer*

Kindness
One of the most difficult things to give away is kindness – it is usually returned. *Anonymous*

Laziness
Anybody who isn't pulling his weight is probably pushing his luck. *Anonymous*

Life
Life is what happens to you when you're making other plans. *Robert Balzer*

Love

Give her two red roses, each with a note. The first note says: 'For the woman I love', and the second: 'For my best friend.' *Anonymous*

Love is composed of a single soul inhabiting two bodies. *Aristotle, 4th century BC philosopher*

Love is a blazing, crackling green-wood flame, as much smoke as flame; friendship, married friendship particularly, is a steady, intense, comfortable fire. Love, in courtship is friendship in hope; in matrimony, friendship upon proof. *Samuel Richardson, 17th century English novelist*

Marriage

A good marriage is like a casserole, only those responsible for it really know what goes in it. *Anonymous*

There is no more lovely, friendly and charming relationship, communion or company than a good marriage. *Martin Luther, 15th century German reformer.*

All marriages are happy. It's living together afterwards that is difficult. *Anonymous*

Marriage is like a cage; one sees the birds outside desperate to get in; and those inside desperate to get out. *Michel de Montaigne, 16th century French writer*

I've been married so many times my certificate now reads: 'To whom it may concern.' *Mickey Rooney, 20th century American actor*

Better to have loved a short man than never to have loved a tall. *Anonymous*

An archaeologist is the best husband a woman can have; the older she gets the more interested he is in her. *Agatha Christie, 20th century English author*

Marriage is like a bank account. You put it in, you take it out, you lose interest. *Irwin Corey, 20th century American humorist*

Marriage is not a ritual or an end. It is a long, intricate, intimate dance together and nothing matters more than your own sense of balance and your choice of partner. *Amy Bloom, 20th century psychotherapist*

Marriage is a matter of give and take, but so far I haven't been able to find anybody who'll take what I have to give. *Cass Daley, 20th century American comedienne*

Every mother generally hopes that her daughter will snag a better husband than she managed to do...but she's certain that her boy will never get as great a wife as his father did. *Anonymous*

Marriage is like a violin. After the music is over, you still have the strings. *Anonymous*

Marriage resembles a pair of shears, so joined that they cannot be separated; often moving in opposite directions, yet always punishing any one who comes between them. *Sydney Smith, 19th century English preacher*

Public speaking
It usually takes me more than three weeks to prepare a good impromptu speech. *Mark Twain, 19th century American author and humorist*

Second marriage
I'm not so old, and not so plain, and I'm quite prepared to marry again. *W.S. Gilbert, 20th century English playwright and humorist*

Self-deprecating
I will try to follow the advice that a university president once gave a prospective commencement speaker. 'Think of yourself as the body at an Irish wake,' he said. 'They need you in order to have the party, but no-one expects you to say very much.' *Anthony Lake, 20th century US National Security advisor*

Toasts
A toast to sweethearts. May all sweethearts become married couples and may all married couples remain sweethearts. *Anonymous*

Here's to the bride and groom. May their happiness last forever and may we be fortunate enough to continue being part of it. *Anonymous*

I wish you health; I wish you wealth; I wish you gold in store; I wish you heaven when you die; what could I wish you more? *Anonymous*

Index